INTERMEDIATE PIANO DUET

1 PIANO, 4 HANDS

CONTEMPORARY
WORSHIP DUETS

ARRANGED BY BILL WOLAV

ISBN 978-1-61780-391-8

HAL•LEONARD®
CORPORATION

7777 W. BLUEMOUND RD. P.O. BOX 13819 MILWAUKEE, WI 53213

Visit Hal Leonard Online at
www.halleonard.com

AGNUS DEI

SECONDO

Words and Music by
MICHAEL W. SMITH

AGNUS DEI

PRIMO

Words and Music by
MICHAEL W. SMITH

SECONDO

PRIMO

PRIMO

BE UNTO YOUR NAME

SECONDO

Words and Music by LYNN DeSHAZO
and GARY SADLER

BE UNTO YOUR NAME

PRIMO

Words and Music by LYNN DeSHAZO
and GARY SADLER

SECONDO

SECONDO

PRIMO

HE IS EXALTED

SECONDO

Words and Music by
TWILA PARIS

HE IS EXALTED

PRIMO

Words and Music by
TWILA PARIS

With energy

SECONDO

PRIMO

HERE I AM TO WORSHIP

SECONDO

Words and Music by
TIM HUGHES

HERE I AM TO WORSHIP

PRIMO

Words and Music by
TIM HUGHES

Flowing

mp

SECONDO

PRIMO

SECONDO

PRIMO

I WILL RISE

SECONDO

Words and Music by CHRIS TOMLIN,
JESSE REEVES, LOUIE GIGLIO
and MATT MAHER

I WILL RISE

PRIMO

Words and Music by CHRIS TOMLIN,
JESSE REEVES, LOUIE GIGLIO
and MATT MAHER

Moderately

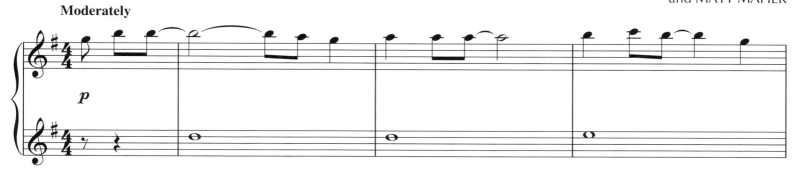

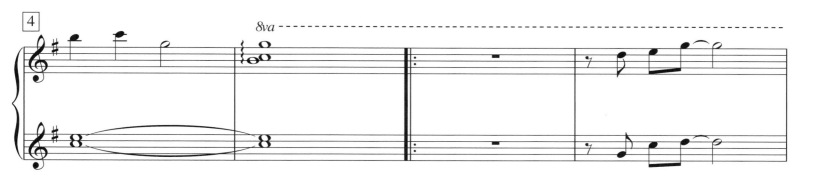

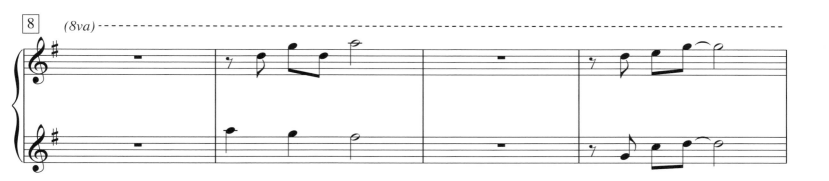

SECONDO

SECONDO

THE POTTER'S HAND

SECONDO

Words and Music by
DARLENE ZSCHECH

THE POTTER'S HAND

PRIMO

Words and Music by
DARLENE ZSCHECH

SECONDO

PRIMO

SECONDO

REVELATION SONG

SECONDO

Words and Music by
JENNIE LEE RIDDLE

REVELATION SONG

PRIMO

Words and Music by
JENNIE LEE RIDDLE

SECONDO

PRIMO

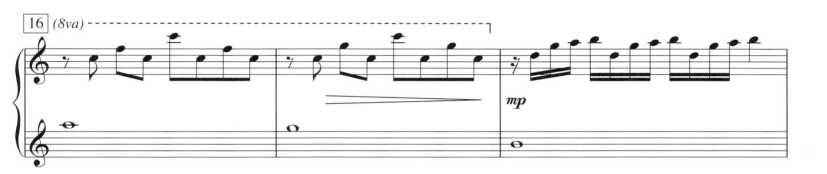

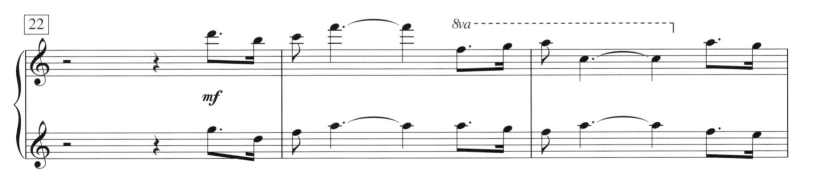

YOUR NAME

SECONDO

Words and Music by PAUL BALOCHE
and GLENN PACKIAM

YOUR NAME

PRIMO

Words and Music by PAUL BALOCHE
and GLENN PACKIAM

SECONDO

SECONDO

PRIMO

The Best
PRAISE & WORSHIP
Songbooks for Piano

Above All
THE PHILLIP KEVEREN SERIES
15 beautiful praise song piano solo arrangements by Phillip Keveren. Includes: Above All • Agnus Dei • Breathe • Draw Me Close • He Is Exalted • I Stand in Awe • Step by Step • We Fall Down • You Are My King (Amazing Love) • and more.
00311024 Piano Solo.................................$11.95

The Best Praise & Worship Songs Ever
80 all-time favorites: Awesome God • Breathe • Days of Elijah • Here I Am to Worship • I Could Sing of Your Love Forever • Open the Eyes of My Heart • Shout to the Lord • We Bow Down • dozens more.
00311057 P/V/G $22.99

Modern Hymns
NEW CLASSICS FOR TODAY'S WORSHIPPER
Piano/vocal/guitar arrangements of 20 worship favorites: Amazing Grace (My Chains Are Gone) • How Deep the Father's Love for Us • In Christ Alone • Take My Life • The Wonderful Cross • and more.
00311739 P/V/G $14.95

More of the Best Praise & Worship Songs Ever
76 more contemporary worship favorites, including: Beautiful One • Everlasting God • Friend of God • How Great Is Our God • In Christ Alone • Let It Rise • Mighty to Save • Your Grace Is Enough • more.
00311800 P/V/G $24.99

Everlasting God
Our matching folio includes: Beautiful One • Everlasting God • Holy Is the Lord • Hosanna • In Christ Alone • Lord, Reign in Me • We Fall Down • You Never Let Go • and more.
00311790 P/V/G $14.95

51 Must-Have Modern Worship Hits
A great collection of 51 of today's most popular worship songs, including: Amazed • Better Is One Day • Everyday • Forever • God of Wonders • He Reigns • How Great Is Our God • Offering • Sing to the King • You Are Good • and more.
00311428 P/V/G $22.99

Piano Interludes for Worship
by David Ritter
This songbook is designed to offer musical support and a soothing ambiance for various aspects of the worship service, such as Communion, Prayer, Scripture Reading, Invitation, etc. 14 original pieces, including: Ambiance • Consecration • Devotion • Passion • Pensive • Reflection • Sanctus • and more.
00311472 Piano Solo...................................$9.95

Praise & Worship Duets
THE PHILLIP KEVEREN SERIES
8 worshipful duets by Phillip Keveren: As the Deer • Awesome God • Give Thanks • Great Is the Lord • Lord, I Lift Your Name on High • Shout to the Lord • There Is a Redeemer • We Fall Down.
00311203 Piano Duet $11.95

Shout to the Lord!
THE PHILLIP KEVEREN SERIES
14 favorite praise songs, including: As the Deer • El Shaddai • Give Thanks • Great Is the Lord • How Beautiful • More Precious Than Silver • Oh Lord, You're Beautiful • A Shield About Me • Shine, Jesus, Shine • Shout to the Lord • Thy Word • and more.
00310699 Piano Solo $12.95

The Chris Tomlin Collection
15 songs from one of the leading artists and composers in Contemporary Christian music, including the favorites: Be Glorified • Holy Is the Lord • How Can I Keep from Singing • How Great Is Our God • Indescribable • Not to Us • Take My Life • We Fall Down • and more.
00306951 P/V/G $16.99

Worship Songs & Stories
Text by Lindsay Terry
This collection features PVG music plus the inspiring and intriguing stories behind 20 beloved praise & worship songs. Includes: Blessed Be Your Name • Days of Elijah • Forever • God of Wonders • He Is Exalted • Holy Is the Lord • I Stand in Awe • There Is None Like You • We Fall Down • and more.
00311478 P/V/G $14.95

Worship – The Ultimate Collection
Matching folio with 24 top worship favorites, including: Blessed Be Your Name • Draw Me Close • God of Wonders • He Reigns • Here I Am to Worship • I Could Sing of Your Love Forever • Lord, Reign in Me • Open the Eyes of My Heart • Yesterday, Today and Forever • and more.
00313337 P/V/G $17.95

Worship Together Piano Solo Favorites
A dozen great worship songs tastefully arranged for intermediate piano solo. Includes: Amazing Grace (My Chains Are Gone) • Beautiful Savior (All My Days) • Facedown • The Heart of Worship • How Great Is Our God • and more.
00311477 Piano Solo $12.95

Worship Without Words
arr. Ken Medema
The highly creative Ken Medema has arranged 13 worship songs and classic hymns, perfect for blended worship. Includes: As the Deer • I Could Sing of Your Love Forever • Open the Eyes of My Heart • You Are My All in All • and more.
00311229 Piano Solo $12.95

FOR MORE INFORMATION, SEE YOUR LOCAL MUSIC DEALER,
OR WRITE TO:

HAL•LEONARD®
CORPORATION
7777 W. BLUEMOUND RD. P.O. BOX 13819 MILWAUKEE, WI 53213

www.halleonard.com

P/V/G = Piano/Vocal/Guitar Arrangements

Prices, contents, and availability subject to change without notice.

0810